MOMmy

Book Cover by Knot E. Nuff

Illustrations by Knot E. Nuff

Formatting by Knot E. Nuff

Published by Rerolling Human Publishing (owned by Knot E. Nuff)

Visit the Author and Publisher's website at: rerollinghuman.com (website made by Knot E. Nuff)

The story, all names, characters, and incidents portrayed in this production are fictitious. No identification with actual persons (living or deceased), places, buildings, and products is intended or should be inferred. The author is a big fat liar and made everything up because they are mean.

Typesets: Didot Title, Underdog, Libre Caslon Display, Arial Narrow, Overpass

First edition 2024 ISBN: 979-8-9917840-3-0 (paperback) I 979-8-9917840-2-3 (e-book)

MOMmy

The First Perennial Issue

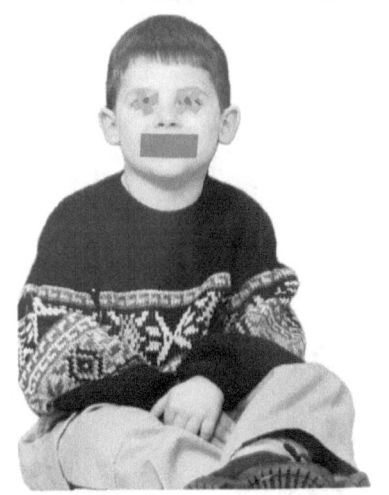

by Knot E. Nuff

(Chapbook)

All 3 of My Children Are Dead
My Son is Mean
It's My Daughter's Fault My Other Son is Dead

Dead.
Mean.
M - r - - r - r?

Dear Ken's Dad,

Do you believe in love
            at first sight?

Do you believe in soul mates?
Do you believe in marriage?

Do you believe a son
should protect himself

                                    from his parents?

Do you believe a son
should protect the neighbors

                                    from his mother?

Do you believe a son,
once gifted a backpack,
should be happy to learn

                        alone

Do you believe a son
dreams to pack and carry
bookmarks and paperweights

                                    Do you believe a son
                                should protect his father
from his mother?

                                    Do you believe a son
                                should believe a father
would believe his son?

                                    Do you believe a son
                                should believe a Father
when lies are all he's given

                                    to believe in?

Do you believe it?

your son.

he's *thirty*.

Does he believe in love?

Do you know when he might
see it for the first time?

Just curious.

it's really not all that important,

A Former Roommate

Table of Contents

"Look at him! So happy with so little," fetishizing the man who laughs in zoo cages. He never whimpers;
not with monkey or bird, elephant or giraffe, lions and sharks.
He's not picky.

Unless, of course, you're asking his mother.

if Dogs owned humans
would you beg
for treat

ment?

expect: *good*
human!
when you cry
wolf

would tall
tales
tuck?   kicked
off your own
pedestal

'**No!**   *Bad* human!

what did I Bark about

playing Victim
in the house

you built'

2

your cold

runny Nose

smackled.   rubbed.

in your own

Piss

Don't Shoot the Messenger

Behind every great man
is a great woman

If you hate men

blame mothers

Save The Mailmen

Behind every Son
of Sam is a great mommy   wound

If you hate school shootings

ban mothers

I Love Voting Booths, I Love Them Not, I Love Voting Booths, I Love Them Not...

Behind every bold lie
is a scared truth

If you hate voting booths

blame elections

Hot Sauce in Her Purse; Pepper Spray in a Child's Lunchbox

Behind every baby kissed by a grown man
is a politician a woman keeps in her pants

If you hate pedophiles

blame Monica Lewinsky

Hey, Wait a Minute! This Isn't a Popsicle!

Behind every mail in ballot
is a politician trying to get in your pants

If you hate fraud

blame the mail in power

Doesn't have to be the guy who made the law.
or even a politician.

Or in a position of power.

which mail should we shred today?

8

Real World Applications of the Scientific Method for Dummies: Process of Elimination

Let's do your tarot reading.
Pick any.

i'll back you up.

Sorry, He Goes Crazy When He Sees the Mailman I Hate Men Don't Worry Though He's Friendly

Alexandria Octavio-Cortes sponsored that

law? Hm. Must be something to it.

Guess I should look into it more,

it's just so hard to hear
the news over the shredder

10

Petitioning For dB Limitations

blame paper shredder manufacturers

11

Salt<Fresh<Well<Tap<Filtered<Bottled<Purified<Spring
<Smart<pH balanced<LiquidDeath

Behind every rehydrated scam
is a shriveling truth

If you hate ocean waste

ban water

Aquafina

Behind every bottle in the ocean
is someone who loves water

If you hate people who litter

blame thirst

I Only Drink Like… 2 Cans Of Soda A Day. Diet. For the Taste

Behind every Pacific 6pack plastic packaging is someone who donates 99% of their fortune to charity

If you care about strangled turtles

why aren't you separating your bottles from your cans, removing the caps, making sure the plastic is clean, checking to see which kind of plastic this plastic is(some plastics can't be recycled{don't forget companies change sometimes so make sure you do this with every piece of plastic you use, every time[make sure you check local ordinances first because each township handles it differently| if they don't have good processes in place why aren't you lobbying your local politicians|]}), and paying for a service that actually disposes of waste properly(make sure you do your research, a lot of them greenwash to make a profit)

Fire USPS

I'm not me on stage
i'mother

If you hate my poems

blameothers

Return Policy?

Behind every unwanted delivery
is a mom
-my wound

If i'm making you uncomfortable

blame Mother

She'll blame my Dad

or i never act like this when he's around
or he's never around
or "My own son hates me because you just try to be his friend"
or it's weird that a son would hug his dad. you both look like

       faggots.

                   (someone else said that)

she won't tell me who 'cause then i might not like that person and

       they're just trying to help

i know how i am. i'm
              so critical for a 7 year old.

she's just letting me know so i don't embarrass her in front of friends

or no she said that so i don't embarrass myself in front of my friends
or i have selective hearing
or she doesn't remember saying that
or she'd never say that
or i know that's not what she meant
or that's not what she said
or i know that's not what she said

or

you   or

you

don't remember

or that one lady from the grocery store who never rang me up right because she's jealous of how smart you are you remember her right? you don't remember that time when you somehow got lost when you were 6 you didn't get in the car and I left while you were still in the store holding me up and when I found you she had you and you were crying? because she must have been mean to you or something and that's why you're like this. or you were crying because you were trying to make me feel bad about that one time you didn't like the grocery store cake I bought for your birthday because I love chocolate. is that why you're like this? you try to make me feel bad that's why you don't like chocolate cake you remember that right?

you don't remember that time when I and I and **you** because **you** mean! me me and why **you** remember?

you   or
you don't remember that time when or
you don't remember that time or
you don't remember you or
you don't remember time
you don't remember or
you don't time
you don't
    don't time
    don't you
    don't

Lost And/Or/But Not

i have trouble showing empathy for people who
lost Mothers

i'm supposed to act like their situation is worse
than mine

But i'm often jealous of what things would have
been like

If i never had to learn my Mother was the way
She is

If i never had to not trust family: i don't know who
is who

If i never had to learn that i wasn't good enough
for good

If i never had to learn that any strength i find, i
should hide

If i never had to learn that nothing i do is what
i should've

If i never had to live through development of
consciousness

She hated that.
my conscience.

If i fantasize what it would be like if She died
postpartum

If i never had to learn to pump Her gas
at four

She used me.

Until She couldn't.

Then She hated me.

Until i could do it for Her.

If i learn they had a Mother. It must be "at least i have one"

If i never: She's right, you know. the name She gave you;

Scorn. Scorn. Scorn. Scorn. Scorn. Scorn. Scorn. Scorn. Scorn. Scorn. Scorn. Scorn. Scorn. Scorn. Scorn. asshole. Scorn. Scorn. Scorn. wimp. Scorn. bully. Scorn. Scorn. Scorn. mean. Scorn. Scorn. Scorn. Scorn. Scorn. Scorn. Scorn. Scorn. Scorn. Scorn. Scorn. lonely. Scorn. ungrate. broken. Scorn. ful. Scorn Scorn! Scorn. Scorn. Scorn. Scorn. Scorn   Scorn. Scorn. Scorn. Scorn.

Scorn.

of shit. Scorn. Scorn. Scorn   crybaby. Scorn. intolerant. Scorn. Scorn. Scorn. Scorn. Scorn. Scorn. Scorn. lazy. Scorn. faggot. homophobe. Scorn. liar. Scorn. Scorn. Scorn. Scorn. Scorn. Scorn. Scorn. Scorn. Scorn. Scorn. weird. Scorn. arrogant. Scorn. Scorn. Scorn. Scorn. Scorn. Scorn. Scorn. Scorn. Scorn. Scorn. Scorn. Scorn. Scorn. Scorn. Scorn. Scorn. Scorn. Scorn. Scorn. regret. Scorn. Scorn. Scorn. Scorn. Scorn. Scorn. Scorn. Scorn. Scorn. Scorn. Scorn. Scorn. Scorn. king. Scorn. Scorn. Scorn. Scorn. Scorn. Scorn. Scorn. Scorn. Scorn. Scorn. Scorn. Scorn. Scorn.

if i never had to live through
if i

10/3

in the attic is where my brother died
buried in angles, six feet
when the gutters were generous
when his eyes were six teen
when his feet should throttle
     permit

my mother pulled the emergency
vocal cord. shut him the *fuck* up
flushed her putrid voice thru Mic
bitching "I'm Failure. I'll have two
inches from a roof. tap tap.   Santa?
deer in triggerlight. tap tap. two
fingers tying ribbon. tap tap. two
rubber rabbit ears.
          knock knock

     I'll have two hundred grams."

when my age was 19, my brother dropped
when his age was 31, my brother dropped
in a basement.   lips white   kiss mother
                    fucker.

when my age was 4 , my brother died
when his age was 16, my brother died
in the attic.   lips white   crack step
                    father.

my age is 3de
adagemybrotherlipswhitemother
'shusbandstillhelping her pull
emergencycordbra
kesabusementin
debasement of a
basement of her
in my brother in
vein in casket in
vain in my throat
in an attic and 4

at least it was his
step
        step

step father letting
my bmymy b
my biology helping
my my bio

DAD. STOP.

                    her murder children

My Mother, I Call Her Mat'er

'caretakers! Need Care. takers?'
a donation Crier. staked on a corner
bookstorefront "Da'ter's Nook"

at the crossing of Jesus
Road, Yellow Rose, red light
HIGH VOLTAGE red light and

                                                NO

                                            TURNS

a new leaf
-let paper

i'm hanging
from Mat'er
's closed door
policy

while she tells the(any) friend
ly mailman "Da'ter is so imp
ortant, she's the Maskot." **the**
Allure. the Store
front poster,   hung

         "come, in   ;   **in, come"**
      splatter-type   white-face
        script   **"open 7 days!**
              5pm-9am!"

         A   bold text bust through the buttonholes -
     A   bosom betrayed by broken buttons -
  A   blessed blossom; accursed by beauty -   to beckon;

"It's quiet in here" spur saddlestitched-lips

"We accept donors" beg engraved palm-lines

"We accept *all* donors." repeat ripped Mom-jeans

"Help" my left stigma

"Me-" my right stye

"Stay Open"

legs

Beware of C@-h- @--'s
who sign their name

'different'

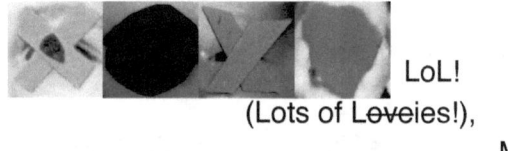 LoL!
(Lots of Loveies!),

Mom

Hi 'my!

Is this what you meant when you said I should be more like other kids?

you   don't remember?   or

          you thought you didn't say?

look at how **they** treat **their**
They do everything for
They worship

Want to   **immortalize**

Well... **I**   hope   **this** is what you meant!   because-

Future Releases:

- **S_____ss** (full-length poetry book)
- _____ (other issues)

Follow me on:

This QR code (and link) below will bring you to a "linktree"

It contains links to all of my social media and online presence:

https://linktr.ee/
RerollingHuman

- X (formerly Twitter)
- Instagram
- Website and Newsletter
- Youtube
- Tiktok
- Twitch
- Threads
- Bluesky
- Facebook

Author Biographies

v1:
Knot E. Nuff was a good boy, his mother's "bulldog," until he became mean and started bullying his mother around the age of 3. he stopped speaking to his mother in 2020 to be extra mean.

v2:
Knot E. Nuff was a good boy, his mother's "bulldog," until he became mean and started bullying his mother around the age of 6. they still talk all the time. he just doesn't say much, because you know how he is. he still works at [sexy corporation to work at]. isn't that so cool? no sorry she can't tell him you said hello, he's busy.

v3:
Knot E. Nuff was a good boy, his mother's "bulldog," until nothing happened at all and his mother just can't understand why he won't talk to her anymore. she's worried. if you talk to him, can you please tell him to call?

v4:
Knot E. Nuff was a good boy, his mother's "bulldog," until he became mean and started bullying his mother around the age of 7. he stopped speaking to his mother in 2018 because he's been sadistic since he was 10. it's because his mother's other son (VERY IMPORTANT: NOT HIS BROTHER, JUST HER SON) died. he likes twisting the knife. and his sister [pick a card, any card]. now all her children are dead. his mother never did anything wrong. why is the world out to get her?

v5:
reserved for future. If his mother hears of and/or reads this book, this page will be updated with the most current and convenient truth-set. truth will be distributed via flying monkey. upon receipt, you must destroy any and all evidence and/or memory of past versions. you will be expected to plea guilty.
(you know what for, don't play dumb)

v1:

reserved for future [something about a book to punish her] [some form of triangulation] [something about things being the way they are because they were planned since adolescence so that this book could be written] [something about not truth] [potentially attempt to play nonchalant] [and many more! collect them all!]

v2:

reserved for future truth amendments

v3:

reserved for future truth amendments

v4:

reserved for future truth amendments

v5:

reserved for future truth amendments

In A ~~Year~~ Fever Dream   To: Dad[1]
your boots will reek and decay
expired milk rotting
where a sole should be, but isn't
in the junkyard it belongs in. yet

you always wore your shoes longer
than you should. until you can't stand
up to it. but now you have new ones
that light up every time you step

into a room - their faces smiling
to be worn again. you'll be embarrassed
to think you can run faster
but it will be true

on labor day, you'll be late; K---- will drive
you up a wall. "The food's getting cold"
'who gives a shit
it's just another day'

just like every other year
except it's the first year
you'll celebrate
in 34 years

you'll see B--- and B---   (and $%#, i guess)
talk to K---- and K-----   (S------ *might* say something)
while you sit with –z- and Z--   (you'll meet their dog too)
and i show up even later than you   (i always do)

you'll know your second granddaughter
for almost a year
and her age will be a year

but she'll almost be two

but there will still be milk
in the fridge

the only difference is
someone will pour

a glass

For You

Narcissistic Abuse Hotline

website: www.thehotline.org

call: 1.800.799.SAFE (7233)

text: send "START" to 88788

visit the website for the most accurate information

Thank you

so much for reading. I cannot fully express how much it means to me that you've made it this far. While I deeply appreciate every reader and hope the experience resonated with you, my ultimate goal is to reach and support victims of narcissistic abuse—especially those who suffered or suffer at the hands of their own mothers. Emotional abuse is devastating in any form, but in my experience, maternal abuse is particularly isolating. It happens during your most formative years, in the context of a society that often denies the possibility that a mother could harm her own child.

This widespread denial compounds the trauma, leading gaslit children to endure further, unimaginable pain. I cannot tell you how many times I heard things like, "You must be misunderstanding; a mother would never say that to her child," or "You should love your mother." For years, I believed both of these statements. I thought I was the problem—until I became an adult, severed ties, and, later, understood the factors at play. All I ever wanted was to be loved for who I was. Unfortunately, being anything other than an extension of my mother was an affront to be punished.

The poems in this book are written for me, but they are published for those who need to hear that you are not the problem—that your experience, pain, and anger, is real and valid. I hope my work gives you the confidence to protect yourself (healthily), even if no one else will. Because I wish someone had done that for me. Because I wish someone had done that for my brother.

My hope is to help as many people as possible—but I can't do it alone. If my words have resonated with you, I would be so grateful if you could support my mission by submitting an honest review on platforms like Amazon or Goodreads. Please share this book or anything you gained from it with anyone who might find value in it.

Thank you again, from the bottom of my heart.

Still,
Knot E. Nuff

42

[1] (Fictional) Character Background: Keeps shoes for 20+ years and only gets new ones when duct tape can no longer save them. Worked at the same milk-related business for a very long time.

Couldn't find a pair of balls while watching the lottery on Football Sunday at a bowling alley next to a juggler's convention. Rather than making a difficult decision, would rather watch their son make far more difficult decisions; sacrificing everything to protect himself.

Meanwhile, inadvertently expects other people he loves to accept abuse in order to keep him a part of their life. This makes sense, of course: to do anything other than protect an abusive person at all costs would be mean.

In mathematical terms:

(son+daughter+sister+nephew+grandson+granddaughter+great-grand-daughters+friends+security+hobbies+values+self) < ((master-wife(emotional abuse+ (physical assault*many)+financial abuse)/(cognitive dissonance+slavery))*0

SYNONYMS: Host. Meal Ticket. Enabler. Brainwashed. Complicit. Weak. Flying Monkey. Working On it (for 20+years). Truth-Silencer. Nice guy, though.

LIES: Knows What Is Best. Not Protecting Master - Protecting *Others* from Master!!!! Living a Full Life. Does What is Right. Fearless. Insert: [Anything Needed to Protect Master]. Gets it.

www.ingramcontent.com/pod-product-compliance
Lightning Source LLC
Chambersburg PA
CBHW050907120626
46554CB00003B/1066